Wild World

Watching Reindeer
in Europe

Elizabeth Miles

Heinemann
LIBRARY

www.heinemann.co.uk/library

Visit our website to find out more information about Heine

To order:

 Phone 44 (0) 1865 888066

Send a fax to 44 (0) 1865 314091

 Visit the Heinemann Bookshop at www.heinemann.co.u

and order online.

First published in Great Britain by Heinemann Library, Halley Court, Jordan Hill, Oxford OX2 8EJ, part of Harcourt Education. Heinemann is a registered trademark of Harcourt Education Ltd.

Editorial: Nancy Dickmann and Sarah Chappelow
Design: Ron Kamen and edesign
Illustrations: Martin Sanders
Picture Research: Maria Joannou and Christine Martin
Production: Camilla Crask
Originated by Modern Age
Printed and bound in Italy by Printer Trento srl

ISBN 0 431 19068 2
10 09 08 07 06
10 9 8 7 6 5 4 3 2 1

British Library Cataloguing in Publication Data
Miles, Elizabeth
Watching reindeer in Europe. – (Wild world)
599.6'5817'0948
A full catalogue record for this book is available from the British Library.

Acknowledgements
The Publishers would like to thank the following for permission to reproduce the following photographs: Alamy pp. 23 (Chris Wallace), 27 (B & C Alexander); Ardea p. 24; Bruce Coleman p. 12 (Allan G Potts); Corbis pp. 4 (Staffan Widstrand), 5, 18 (M Warford); FLPA pp. 9 (Jim Brandenburg), 11 (Yva Momatiuk), 13 (Michio Hoshino), 14 (Helen Rhode), 15 (Robert Canis), 28 (Tui de Roy); Getty Images pp. 21, 25; Nature PL p. 16 (Asgeir Helgestad), 17 (Asgeir Helgestad), 20 (Asgeir Helgestad), 26 (David Tipling); NHPA pp. 7 (Laurie Campbell), 19 (B & C Alexander), 22 (B & C Alexander); PhotoLibrary.com pp. 8 (Mark Hamblin), 10 (Owen Newman). Cover photograph of reindeer reproduced with permission of Nature Picture Library/Asgeir Helgestad.

The publishers would like to thank Michael Bright of the BBC Natural History Unit for his assistance in the preparation of this book.

Every effort has been made to contact copyright holders of any material reproduced in this book. Any omissions will be rectified in subsequent printings if notice is given to the publishers. The paper used to print this book comes from sustainable resources.

Contents

Words written in bold, **like this**, are explained in the glossary.

Meet the reindeer

This is Europe, the home of reindeer. A reindeer is a type of deer. Deer are **mammals**. They are the only animals with **antlers** on their heads.

▼ *A reindeer's antlers are made of bone.*

There are more than 30 different kinds of deer. Some deer are small and others are large. Their antlers come in different shapes.

Moose are the largest type of deer.

Europe: the cold north

Reindeer live in the most northern parts of Europe, North America, and Asia. They live in **tundra**, forests, and mountains. In North America, reindeer are called caribou.

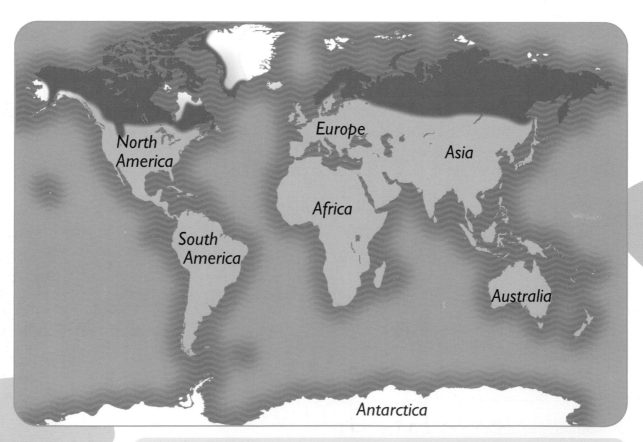

North America

Europe

Asia

Africa

South America

Australia

Antarctica

Key ● *This colour shows where reindeer live in Europe, North America, and Asia.*

It is cold for most of the year in northern Europe, but a reindeer's thick fur keeps it warm. Sometimes there is little to eat in the icy tundra.

🔺 *Reindeer have big hooves for walking in the snow.*

There's a reindeer!

This is a **male** reindeer in autumn. His darker summer **coat** is changing into a paler, thicker coat for winter. Male reindeer are called bulls.

▶▶ *This male reindeer is taller than you.*

large antlers

thick coat

wide hooves

Female reindeer are called cows. They are smaller than bulls (males).

Males often live on their own. **Females** stay in **herds**. Female reindeer are the only female deer to have **antlers**.

Reindeer food

In autumn, reindeer eat mushrooms, grasses, **lichen**, and leaves from bushes and trees. There is little else to eat in this cold northern forest area.

▼ *These reindeer are **herbivores** which means they eat plants.*

The reindeer eat grasses and leaves all morning. They do not chew their food much. Later, the food travels back up into their mouths so they can chew it more.

▲ *When reindeer chew their food a second time, it is called chewing the cud.*

The rut

Autumn is the **rutting** season. The strongest **male** reindeer use their **antlers** to fight for **females**. Each male fights for five to fifteen females.

⏫ Antlers are very strong. A reindeer could get badly hurt.

The male **mates** with the females he has won. His group of females is called a harem. The females will have **calves** in spring.

⬆ *The male calls the females to him with three loud grunts.*

Antlers

After the **rutting** season, the **males** shed their **antlers**. New ones will grow in spring. **Females** shed theirs in spring. Their new ones grow straight away.

▼ *Antlers have a covering that rubs off before they are shed.*

The old antlers are left on the ground. Some reindeer eat them.

In autumn and winter the females need their antlers. They use them to keep male reindeer away. Males are not as powerful without their antlers.

Living in the snow

Snow falls in the winter. The reindeer's wide hooves stop it from getting stuck in the deep snow.

▼ *A reindeer uses a hoof to paw through the snow to find **lichen** to eat.*

The reindeer's fur **coat** keeps it warm and dry, even in winter. Its nose has a special pad. The pad stops the reindeer getting **frostbite**.

◀◀ *While **grazing**, the reindeer's nose is stuck in the snow all the time.*

On the move

After a long winter in the forest, reindeer **migrate** further **north**. They go to the **tundra**. The snow has melted and there are grasses and plants to eat.

▼ *Reindeer's strong legs help them travel long distances.*

🔺 *Reindeer usually walk or trot. Sometimes they may jump or run.*

The reindeer migrate in a large **herd**. The journey takes a long time. They follow the same path every year.

Calving

During the spring **migration** some **female** reindeer leave the **herd**. They are going to have their **calves**. Each female gives birth to one calf.

⏶ *A calf can walk just an hour after it is born.*

An hour after their birth, the calves follow their mothers back to the herd. Staying with the herd keeps the calves safe from **predators**, such as wolves.

▼ *Two-day-old calves can keep up with the herd.*

Growing up

The young **calves** live off their mother's milk for several weeks. Soon they will learn to eat the same food as their mother.

▲ *This calf is drinking its mother's milk.*

The calves have started to grow their first set of **antlers**. The antlers are covered in a thin, soft skin called velvet.

▶▶ A calf's antlers are soft and easily hurt.

Finding food

The reindeer spend the summer on the **tundra**. Grass grows slowly there. When the reindeer finish eating the grass in one place, they must move on to find more.

▼ *Reindeer may have to travel a long way to find plants to* **graze** *on.*

▲ *When it gets too cold and windy in the **north**, the reindeer must go back south.*

As autumn comes, the reindeer gather in bigger **herds** to **migrate** again. They are going back to where they were for the autumn **rutting** season.

Reindeer in danger

Some of the forests where reindeer used to **migrate** to have been cut down. If there are no forests, there is no food for the reindeer when they arrive.

▲ *When trees are cut down, there is less **lichen** for reindeer to eat.*

People are trying to save the places where reindeer migrate. That way the reindeer can go safely back to their **rutting** ground each year.

🔺 *In some parts of Europe reindeer are kept by farmers. They do not live in the wild.*

Tracker's guide

When you want to watch animals in the wild, you need to find them first. You can look for clues they leave behind. You can also listen — reindeer legs make a clicking noise as they move.

▲ *Reindeer leave clear tracks on the ground.*

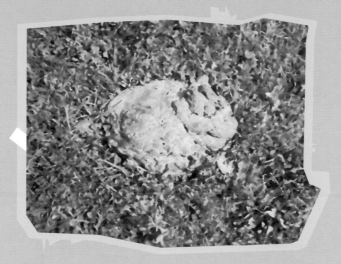

In winter, reindeer droppings are black or brown. In summer they are brownish yellow, like this.

You might be lucky enough to find an **antler** that has been shed.

Glossary

antler bone that sticks out of a deer's head

calves young reindeer, one is called a calf

coat outer covering of fur

female animal that can become a mother when it is grown up. Girls and women are female people.

frostbite when part of a body freezes

graze eat grass

herbivore animal that eats plants

herd group of large, grass-eating animals

lichen small, low plant like moss

male animal that can become a father when it is grown up. Boys and men are male people.

mammal animals that feed their babies their own milk and have some hair on their bodies

mate when male and female animals produce young

migrate travel a long distance, following the same journey every year

north part of the world where it gets very cold

predator animal that catches and eats other animals for food

rutting when male reindeer fight each other for females

tundra flat land where there are few trees and the soil is partly frozen all year

Find out more

Books

Nature's Patterns: Migration, Monica Hughes (Heinemann Library, 2004)

Europe, L. Foster (Heinemann Library, 2002)

Why am I a Mammal? Greg Pyers (Raintree, 2005)

Websites

Find out more about these interesting animals at:

http://www.reindeer.ws/info.htm

Disclaimer

All the internet addresses (URLs) given in this book were valid at the time of going to press. However, due to the dynamic nature of the internet, some addresses may have changed, or sites may have ceased to exist since publication. While the author and publishers regret any inconvenience this may cause readers, no responsibility for such changes can be accepted by either the author(s) or the publishers.

Index

Titles in the *Wild World* series include:

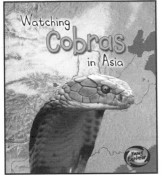

Hardback   0 431 19066 6

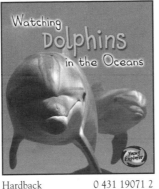

Hardback   0 431 19071 2

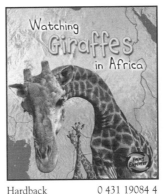

Hardback   0 431 19084 4

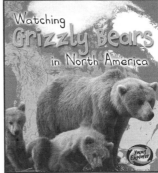

Hardback   0 431 19069 0

Hardback   0 431 19067 4

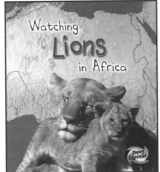

Hardback   0 431 19064 X

Hardback   0 431 19085 2

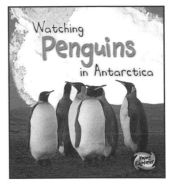

Hardback   0 431 19065 8

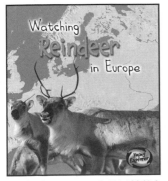

Hardback   0 431 19068 2

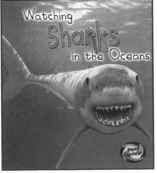

Hardback   0 431 19086 0

Hardback   0 431 19070 4

Find out about other Heinemann Library titles on our website www.heinemann.co.uk/library